APEX PREDATORS
of the Amazon Rain Forest

Jaguar

by Ellen Lawrence

Consultant:

Northern Jaguar Project
Tucson, Arizona

D1710108

BEARPORT PUBLISHING

New York, New York

Credits

Cover, © Shattil & Rozinski/Nature Picture Library; 4T, © Suzi Eszterhaus/Minden Pictures/FLPA; 4B, © Itinerant Lens/Shutterstock; 5, © Patrick Fagot/Biosphoto/FLPA; 6, © Cosmographics; 7TL, © Eye Ubiquitous/Alamy; 7, © Pedro Helder Pinheiro/Shutterstock; 8T, © worldswildlifewonders/Shutterstock; 8B, © Travel Stock/Shutterstock; 9, © Christian Vinces/Shutterstock; 10, © Pete Oxford/Minden Pictures/FLPA; 11, © Michael & Patricia Fogden/Minden Pictures/FLPA; 12T, © Andrea Izzotti/Shutterstock; 12B, © Vadim Petrakov/Shutterstock; 13, © Bruno Pambour/Biosphoto/FLPA; 14, © Luiz Claudio Marigo/Nature Picture Library; 15, © Patricio Robles Gil/Nature Picture Library; 16, © Mark Newman/FLPA; 17, © Nick Gordon/Nature Picture Library; 18T, © ZSSD/Minden Pictures/FLPA; 18B, © Arco Images GmbH/Alamy; 19, © Arco Images GmbH/Alamy; 20, © Patrick Kientz/Biosphoto/FLPA; 21, © Redmond Durrell/Alamy; 22T, © rzstudio/Shutterstock; 22B, © worldswildlifewonders/Shutterstock; 23TL, © Steve Meese/Shutterstock; 23TC, © Ryan Ladbrook/Shutterstock; 23TR, © MyImages-Micha/Shutterstock; 23BL, © Fotos593/Shutterstock; 23BC, © Roger Clark ARPS/Shutterstock; 23BR, © Steve Meese/Shutterstock.

Publisher: Kenn Goin
Editor: Jessica Rudolph
Creative Director: Spencer Brinker
Photo Researcher: Ruby Tuesday Books Ltd

Library of Congress Cataloging-in-Publication Data

Names: Lawrence, Ellen, 1967– , author.
Title: Jaguar / by Ellen Lawrence.
Description: New York, New York : Bearport Publishing, 2017. | Series: Apex
   predators of the Amazon rain forest | Includes bibliographical references
   and index. | Audience: Ages 5 to 8.
Identifiers: LCCN 2016043979 (print) | LCCN 2016050448 (ebook) | ISBN
   9781684020300 (library) | ISBN 9781684020829 (ebook)
Subjects: LCSH: Jaguar—Juvenile literature.
Classification: LCC QL737.C23 L377 2017 (print) | LCC QL737.C23 (ebook) | DDC
   599.75/5—dc23
LC record available at https://lccn.loc.gov/2016043979

For more information, write to Bearport Publishing Company, Inc., 45 West 21st Street, Suite 3B, New York, New York 10010. Printed in the United States of America.

10 9 8 7 6 5 4 3 2 1

Contents

On the Hunt!

It's early morning in the Amazon **rain forest**.

A caiman glides through a muddy river.

Suddenly, a jaguar leaps into the water with a huge splash.

In an instant, the big cat sinks its sharp teeth into the caiman's thick, scaly skin.

The caiman struggles to fight back, but the jaguar is too strong.

caiman

jaguar

4

A jaguar is an apex, or top, **predator**. It hunts many of the animals that share its forest home—but no animals hunt the large cat. Only humans hunt jaguars.

a jaguar attacking a caiman

A Jaguar's Home

Jaguars live in parts of North and South America.

Some jaguars make their homes in rain forests, such as the Amazon.

They live among thick, tangled plants.

These big cats can easily climb trees and often sleep on thick branches.

North America

Atlantic Ocean

Pacific Ocean

South America

N
W   E
S

⬛ Where jaguars live
- - - Amazon rain forest

a jaguar resting on a tree branch

Jaguars stay close to the streams and rivers that flow through the forest. They enter the water to cool off, play, and hunt.

Meet a Jaguar

Jaguars have muscular bodies and short, thick legs.

They are the third largest members of the cat family, after tigers and lions.

A jaguar has yellowish-brown fur.

It has a pattern of light and dark markings called rosettes on its back and sides.

Its head, shoulders, and legs are covered in dark spots.

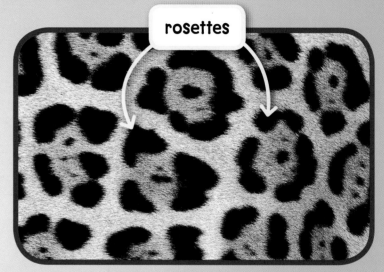

rosettes

spots

How do you think the rosettes and spots on a jaguar's fur help it to hunt?

A male jaguar may weigh up to 200 pounds (91 kg). It measures 6 feet (1.8 m) from its nose to the base of its tail. Female jaguars weigh up to 100 pounds (45 kg) and have shorter bodies.

9

Secret Hunter

A jaguar usually hunts in the early morning or just before dark.

It walks slowly as it listens for **prey**.

The patterns on its fur help it to blend in with the dark forest.

Animals do not see the big cat among the plants and shadows.

Once it spots a meal, the jaguar **stalks**, or creeps up on, its prey.

pads

A jaguar's large paws have soft pads. The pads help it to walk over leaves and twigs without making a sound.

a jaguar blending in with its surroundings

The Attack!

Once a jaguar gets close to its prey, it pounces from its hiding place!

It may leap onto the back of an animal and bite its neck.

It may also crush the skull of its prey with a powerful bite.

Large prey, such as tapirs, deer, and capybaras, can all become a jaguar's meal.

tapir

capybaras

Jaguars also eat monkeys, snakes, frogs, fish, and birds. The cat's sharp teeth can even bite through a turtle's tough shell!

canine tooth

A jaguar's top canine teeth can be 2.5 inches (6.4 cm) long. Is that longer or shorter than your pinky finger?

13

A Powerful Cat

Once a jaguar has killed its prey, it drags the meal to a hidden spot.

This can be tough because the prey is often very heavy.

Sometimes the cat has to pull a large animal like a caiman out of a river.

The jaguar carries the prey in its mouth to some thick bushes.

Then the cat settles down to eat.

a jaguar pulling a caiman from a river

15

Tiny Cubs

Adult jaguars live alone, and males and females only meet up to **mate**.

About 100 days after mating, a female jaguar finds a place that will be her den.

She might choose a cave or a large hole beneath a fallen tree.

Inside the den, she gives birth to two tiny, furry cubs.

The baby jaguars' eyes are closed, and they cannot yet walk.

a pair of jaguars

A Jaguar Family

A mother jaguar feeds her cubs milk from her body.

When she goes hunting, the little cubs stay in the den.

By the time they are three weeks old, their eyes are open and they can walk.

At ten weeks old, the cubs start to explore outside the den and play.

Now, their mother brings them meat to eat.

mother jaguar

three-month-old cubs

a jaguar cub carrying a fish

If one of the cubs wanders too far, the mother jaguar gently picks it up in her mouth and carries it back to the den.

Young Predators

When the cubs are about three months old, they follow their mother when she goes hunting.

The cubs learn how to hunt by watching their mother stalk prey.

At about two years old, the young jaguars leave their mother.

They each find an area of the forest that will be their home **territory**.

Then they begin their grown-up lives as apex predators of the Amazon rain forest!

one-year-old cubs play fighting

How do you think play fighting helps the cubs get ready for their adult life?
(The answer is on page 24.)

Some jaguars are born with black fur. They still have rosettes and spots—the patterns are just harder to see!

21

Science Lab

A jaguar's pattern of rosettes and spots is a type of camouflage (KAM-uh-flahzh). It helps the animal blend in with its surroundings.

Test a Jaguar's Super Spots

You will need:
- A piece of white paper
- Paintbrushes
- Black and dark yellow paint
- A notebook and a pencil

1. Create jaguar fur by painting a piece of paper dark yellow. When the paper is dry, paint rosettes in black.

2. Take your painting outdoors. Choose three different places to hide it, for example in long grass, under a bush in a dark spot, and in the low branches of a tree.

- *Do you think it will be difficult or easy to see the painting in these places? Write your prediction in your notebook.*

3. Place the painting in the first location. Then ask a friend or family member to try to spot the painting.

- *Was it easy or difficult to see? Did your prediction match what you observed?*

4. Hide the painting in the second, then third spots, and ask a friend or family member to find it again.

Science Words

mate (MAYT) to come together to produce young

predator (PRED-uh-tur) an animal that hunts other animals for food

prey (PRAY) an animal that is hunted and eaten by another animal

rain forest (RAYN FORE-ist) a large area of land covered with trees and other plants where lots of rain falls

stalks (STAWKS) slowly creeps up on something while staying hidden

territory (TERR-uh-*tore*-ee) an area of land where an animal finds its food and mates

Index

Read More

Bedoyere, Camilla de la. *The Wild Life of Big Cats (The Wild Side).* New York: Windmill Books (2015).

Ganeri, Anita. *Jaguar (A Day in the Life: Rain Forest Animals).* Chicago: Heinemann-Raintree (2011).

Goldish, Meish. *Bobcat (Desert Animals: Searchin' for Shade).* New York: Bearport (2015).

Learn More Online

To learn more about jaguars, visit **www.bearportpublishing.com/ApexPredators**

About the Author

Ellen Lawrence lives in the United Kingdom. Her favorite books to write are those about nature and animals. In fact, the first book Ellen bought for herself, when she was six years old, was the story of a gorilla named Patty Cake that was born in New York's Central Park Zoo.

Answer for Page 20

Play fighting and wrestling with their brothers and sisters helps young jaguars practice their hunting skills, such as stalking and pouncing, and gets them ready to attack large prey such as caimans.